T0126580

THE LITTLE BOOK OF
FAMOUS
LAST WORDS

Published in 2024 by OH!
An Imprint of Welbeck Non-Fiction Limited,
part of Welbeck Publishing Group.
Offices in: London – 20 Mortimer Street, London W1T 3JW
and Sydney – Level 17, 207 Kent St, Sydney NSW 2000 Australia
www.welbeckpublishing.com

ISBN 978-1-80069-565-8

Compiled and written by: Malcolm Croft
Editorial: Victoria Denne
Project manager: Russell Porter
Production: Jess Brisley

A CIP catalogue record for this book is available from the British Library

Printed in Dubai

10 9 8 7 6 5 4 3 2 1

THE LITTLE BOOK OF
FAMOUS
LAST WORDS

CONTENTS

INTRODUCTION

Welcome to *The Little Book of Famous Last Words*, a celebratory ode to those final phrases notable (and notorious) people have thrown away in the throes of farewell. You know the ones; the legendary last gasps of the world's greatest icons that are so perfect, so unforgettable, that you can't help but applaud in awe.

This terrifically tiny tome is a diverse and definitive collection of history's greatest hits, covering a wealth of characters, good and evil, famous and infamous.

But that's not all. There's more!

Yes, like life and death itself, famous last words can come in all shapes and sizes, and encompass a range of emotions and events.

As well as the funny and unforgettable urgent requests of the sick and dying, we also include a treasure trove of cock-sure (and cock-eyed) pronouncements and prognostications that leave their creators dying on the inside (from embarrassment) – remarks so out of touch that they had to come back to haunt them from the afterlife to eat them.

From funny to sad, good to bad, ironic to moronic, deathbed confessionals to premature celebrations, aphorisms to puns and declarations of love, fear and loathing, this compact com-pendium of famous last words is, well, the last word in famous last words.

Enjoy!

CHAPTER
ONE

HEAVEN'S DOOR

Ladies and gentlemen, let's get this dearly departed party started with the most famous last words ever – at least so far.

This chapter is full of the verbal nails in the metaphorical coffin for many of history's most awesome of icons, who just so happen to be knock-knock-knocking on heaven's door.

I'm losing.

Frank Sinatra, singer and actor, May 14, 1998.

Ol' Blue Eyes died at Cedars-Sinai Medical Hospital, Los Angeles, following a heart attack. His wife, Barbara, at his bedside, had just encouraged him to "keep fighting".

66

I'm shot! I'm shot.*

99

John Lennon, musician, December 8, 1980.

Beatles icon John Lennon was shot multiple times at close range outside The Dakota, his New York apartment building. He stumbled a few steps before collapsing. He was 40 years old.

*His final word is reported to be "Yeah" when asked by a paramedic if he was *the* John Lennon.

I'm bored with it all.

Winston Churchill, UK Prime Minister,
January 24, 1965.

After his seventh stroke put Winston in a coma for two
weeks, he briefly awakened for this final bon mot, before
succumbing to a fatal attack of the heart.

You are wonderful.

Arthur Conan Doyle, author, July 7, 1930.

Infamous fictional detective Sherlock Holmes' famous real-life creator died of a heart attack at the age of 71. His last words were to his wife, Jean, whom he adored immensely.

My God, what's happened?

Diana, Princess of Wales, August 31, 1997.

The People's Princess died in a car crash in the Pont de l'Alma tunnel, Paris. She was escaping pursuing paparazzi. A firefighter overheard her final words before she went into cardiac arrest.

66

I'm going to go and see Jesus.

99

Whitney Houston, singer and actor,
February 11, 2012.

The legendary "I Will Always Love You" singer and
The Bodyguard actor, was found unconscious in a
bathtub at her suite at the Beverly Hilton Hotel,
Los Angeles. Cause of death: accidental drowning.

I'd like to have some milk. Please, please give me some more.

Michael Jackson, musician, June 25, 2009.

The King of Pop had become addicted to propofol, due to increasing insomnia, a drug he called "milk". Hours after taking a lethal dose of propofol, Jackson died. His doctor, Conrad Murray, was found guilty of involuntary manslaughter. He served just two years in prison.

I don't have the passion anymore, and so remember, it's better to burn out than to fade away.

Kurt Cobain, musician, April 8, 1994.

The final line of the Nirvana singer's suicide note. Kurt was found dead in his Seattle home after shooting himself in the head. The line is a nod to the Neil Young song, "My My, Hey Hey (Out of the Blue)".

Why not? After all, it belongs to Him.

Charlie Chaplin, actor and director, December 25, 1977.

Aged 88, Charlie passed away after a stroke took him in his sleep. Earlier that night, a priest attended to him and asked: "May the Lord have mercy on your soul."

I'm going away tonight.

James Brown, musician, December 25, 2006.

On the advice of his dentist, James went to the hospital for observation. Two days later, he passed away from heart failure. His manager, Charles Bobbit, was by his side and heard his last words under laboured breaths.

I'm going to the bathroom to read.

Elvis Presley, musician, August 16, 1977.

Elvis' girlfriend, Ginger Alden, found the singer unresponsive on his bathroom floor. He died of a heart attack caused by a lethal combination of drugs. Alden later revealed Elvis' final words were, "OK, I won't," when she told him, "Don't fall asleep in there."

To the strongest.

Alexander the Great, conqueror and king of
Macedonia, c. June 11, 323 BCE.

Moments before his death, Alexander was asked who
his empire should belong to following his death. Cause
of death? Partying hard.

It is finished.

Jesus Christ, founder of Christianity, c.33 CE.

Jesus Christ died twice. Right before his death by crucifixion, he said it was finished. (It clearly wasn't.) After his resurrection, he ascended to Heaven and said, according to Luke, "Father, into your hands I commit my spirit!"

I am still alive!

Caligula, Roman emperor, January 24, 41 CE.

Rome's most cruel and tyrannical emperor reigned from 37–41 AD. He was murdered and proved wrong.

I hope this exit is joyful and I hope never to return.

Frida Kahlo, artist, July 13, 1954.

Frida, a famous Mexican artist, known for her eye brow lifting self-portraits and pioneering feminism. She died of bronchopneumonia (though suspected overdose). Her last words were attached to her last painting, "Angel of Death".

Ben, make sure you play
'Take My Hand, Precious Lord'
in the meeting tonight. Play it
real pretty.

Martin Luther King, Jr, civil rights leader,
April 4, 1968.

Before Martin stepped out on the second-floor balcony
of the Lorraine Motel in Memphis, Tennessee, he
requested a song from musician friend, Ben Branch, the
hymn "Precious Lord". He never got to hear it – he was
assassinated a minute or so later, at 6.01pm.

All must die. 'Tis enough that the child liveth.

Pocahontas, Native American Ambassador, March 21, 1917.

Pocahontas died at age 20, in Gravesend, England. Her final words were to her husband, John Rolfe, with whom she had a son. Pocahontas became famous for helping English colonists settle in Jamestown, USA, and forging a non-violent relationship between the settlers and her Powhatan tribe.

Irma, I am very sick.

Anne Frank, 1945.

A Jewish victim of the Holocaust, Anne Frank documented
her life in a diary, while she and her family were in hiding
from the Nazis, from 1942 – 1944. When she was arrested,
she was sent to the Bergen-Belsen concentration camp,
where she died of typhus fever. Her last words were to a
friend and survivor, Irma Menkel.

Brothers! Brothers, please!
This is a house of peace!

Malcolm X, freedom fighter and Muslim leader,
February 21, 1965.

After renouncing the Nation of Islam, Malcolm was
gunned down by three NOI assassins as he prepared
to speak at a rally in New York. He was 39. They were
imprisoned for his murder.

"

This is Amelia Earhart! Water's knee deep!

"

Amelia Earhart, the first female to fly solo across the Atlantic Ocean, July 2, 1937.

During an attempt to fly around the world, Amelia, and navigator Fred Noon, disappeared. Coast Guards heard her last words in a distressed SOS radio transmission but dismissed it as a hoax.

Oh wow. Oh wow. Oh wow.

Steve Jobs, founder of Apple, October 5, 2011.

On his deathbed, Steve slipped into eternity surrounded by his children and loved ones. As his breathing slowed, he looked beyond them and repeated these words. "Death didn't happen to Steve," his sister said, "he achieved it."

"
You know, I gotta do it.
"

Aaliyah, musician, August 25, 2001.

Before boarding a plane in the Bahamas, the U.S. singing sensation told her boyfriend that she felt the small plane didn't look safe. He told her not to do it, but she did.

Fuck you.

Tupac Shakur, musician, September 13, 1996.

Tupac was asked by the first police officer at the scene who gunned him down in a drive-by shooting. But Tupac was no rat and took his murderer's identity to his grave. The case was never officially solved.

66

I don't want to die.

99

Amy Winehouse, musician, July 23, 2011.

Found alone and unresponsive at her Camden home,
Amy's toxicology report revealed she died from alcohol
poisoning. The night before she died, she had spoken
with her doctor who recalled her last words, as no one
else has yet shed anymore light. Amy was 27 years old.

Mother, I'm going to get my things and get out of this house. Father hates me and I'm never coming back.

Marvin Gaye, musician, April 1, 1984.

Marvin was shot to death by his father while in a physical altercation with him, and trying to resolve an argument between his parents. He was 44.

I have offended God and mankind because my work did not reach the quality it should have.

Leonardo da Vinci, Italian polymath, May 2, 1519.

Believed, to have died in the arms of French King Francis I, Leonardo's last words are disputed, but these words are a close approximation considering his abilities.

Oh, I am not going to die, am I?
He will not separate us. We have
been so happy.

Charlotte Brontë, author, March 31, 1855.

Esteemed author of *Jane Eyre*, Charlotte spoke these
words to her husband on her deathbed and departed.
Complications from pregnancy a year earlier were the
cause of death. She was 38.

144.

Thomas Fantet de Lagny, French mathematician,
April 11, 1734.

Revered for calculating π to 120 decimal places, on his
deathbed Thomas was asked, "What is the square of 12?"
The answer killed him (but he got it right!)

Ow, fuck!

Roald Dahl, author, November 23, 1990.

"It's just that I will miss you all so much," Roald said to his family on his deathbed. To ease his passing from leukaemia as he slipped into unconsciousness, a nurse injected him with morphine – and one final revolting rhyme sneaked out.

She's comin' on, boys, and she's comin' on strong.

Frank W. "Billy" Tyne Jr., captain of the fishing vessel *Andrea Gail*, October 28, 1991.

Billy's final radio transmission at 6.15pm was the last thing anybody heard from the *Andrea Gail* before it sailed into a perfect storm: the convergence of three massive weather systems in the North Atlantic.

CHAPTER
TWO

THE BENEFIT OF HINDSIGHT

With so much history at our fingertips, it is inevitable that a treasure trove of hilarious hindsight will be found.

As you flick through the next few pages, remember to be kind to the poor sausages who perhaps shouldn't have said the thing they so famously, and confidently, did.

They didn't have the benefit of hindsight that we do now... thankfully!

I'm a fighter not a quitter.

Liz Truss, UK's Prime Minister (for just 44 days),
October 19, 2022.

Liz quit the top job the next day, following a thankfully
short, but calamitous career as PM. Never to be seen
again (?).

66

The internet's completely over, like MTV. At one time MTV was hip and suddenly it became outdated. All these computers and digital gadgets are no good. They just fill your head with numbers and that can't be good for you.

99

Prince, musician, July 2010.

The beloved "Purple Rain" singer got many things right in his life. But this claim was not one of them.

The stocks have reached
what looks like a permanently
high plateau.

Irving Fisher, economist, October 25, 1929.

Irving was the greatest economist in the U.S. Three days
after claiming this expert advice, Wall Street crashed and
burned. The following Great Depression lasted a decade.

66

Y2K is a crisis without precedent
in human history.

99

Edmund X. DeJesus, editor of *BYTE* magazine,
1998.

Edmund's prediction that computer systems would
collapse and planes would fall out of the sky never
happened when January 1, 2000, came – and went –
with zero fuss.

Remote shopping, while entirely feasible, will flop – because women like to get out of the house, like to handle merchandise, like to be able to change their minds.

TIME magazine, 1966.

Thirty years before the advent of Amazon, _TIME_ magazine made a bold prediction about life at the millennium. "We admit it, we got it wrong," they said in 2012.

Television won't be able to hold on to any market it captures after the first six months. People will soon get tired of staring at a plywood box every night

Darryl F. Zanuck, Hollywood studio executive, 1946.

A legend in showbusiness Golden Age, Darryl's words came back to haunt him after televisions instantly became a household name.

I'm going to say this again: I did not have sexual relations with that woman, Miss Lewinsky. I never told anybody to lie, not a single time; never. These allegations are false. And I need to go back to work for the American people.

Bill Clinton, former U.S. President, January 22, 1998.

Bill dug a hole so deep he redefined the very definition of sex, and the word "is", for the American people. He was later impeached for lying under oath.

Read my lips, no new taxes.

George W. Bush, former U.S. President,
August 18, 1988.

As he accepted the Republican nomination for U.S.
president, Dubya Snr. made his most famous remark – a
promise he unfortunately reneged on just two years later.

I am not a crook.

Richard Nixon, former U.S. President,
November 17, 1973.

On this day of infamy, President Richard Nixon denied his
involvement in the Watergate scandal. He was, of course,
a crook.

"

The fundamentals of the
economy are strong.

"

John McCain, former U.S. Senator,
September 15, 2008.

Hours after John made this statement, investment bank
Lehman Brothers filed for bankruptcy – the first domino
to fall in the now-infamous financial crash of 2008. John
was wrong.

Atomic energy might be as good as our present-day explosives, but it is unlikely to produce anything very much more dangerous.

Winston Churchill, former UK Prime Minister, 1939.

The king of quotes, Winston's claim of atomic energy was proven wrong, rather explosively, six years later when the first atomic bombs decimated Japan's Hiroshima and Nagasaki.

Earlier on today, apparently, a woman rang the BBC and said she heard there was a hurricane on the way. Well, if you're watching, don't worry, there isn't!

Michael Fish, weather presenter, October 15, 1987.

Michael has been eating these infamous words since the Great Storm of 1987 knocked the wind out of the UK mere moments after he told millions of viewers no such thing existed.

Almost all of the many predictions now being made about 1996 hinge on the Internet's continuing exponential growth. But I predict the Internet will soon go spectacularly supernova and in 1996 catastrophically collapse.

Robert Metcalfe, founder of 3Com, 1995.

Robert promised to eat his words if he was proved wrong. He was. So, in 1997, at an internet conference, he put the magazine he gave the quote to in a blender... and then ate it in front of a live audience.

66

History is on our side. We will bury you.

99

Nikita Khrushchev, November 18, 1956.

Nikita led the Soviet Union from 1953 to 1964. He famously told the West that Communism's defeat of capitalism was inevitable. He was wrong.

There is no danger that
Titanic will sink. The boat is
unsinkable… and nothing but
inconvenience will be suffered
by the passengers.

Philip Franklin, Vice-President of White Star Line,
April 15, 1912.

Prior to the *Titanic's* maiden voyage, Philip doubled down
on his company's confidence in its mighty ship. A day
later, he reconsidered: "I thought her unsinkable, and I
based my opinion on the best expert advice."

> **"**
> I will be phenomenal to the women. I mean, I want to help women.
> **"**

Donald Trump, former U.S. President and businessman, September 8, 2015.

Before his presidency, Donald made many claims which later bit him on the bottom. After his presidency, he was found guilty of sexual abuse and defamation of one of the many women who charged him with allegations of assault.

Not to mince words, Mr. Epstein, we don't like your boys' sound. Groups of four guitarists are on the way out.

Decca Executive, Decca Records, January 1, 1962.

Exactly who made this claim is often disputed, but someone at Decca said it to Brian Epstein. And boy were they correct. The Beatles were never heard from again. Right?

The only thing different is the hair, as far as I can see. I give them a year.

Ray Bloch, musical director for *The Ed Sullivan Show*, February 9, 1964.

Whatever happens, the U.S.
Navy is not going to be caught
napping.

Frank Knox, Secretary of the Navy, December 4, 1941.

You've guessed it – the then-deadliest attack ever on U.S.
soil, at Pearl Harbor, by more than 350 Japanese airplanes
and bombers, happened (at nap time) three days later.

The horse is here to stay but the automobile is only a novelty – a fad.

George Peck, president of the Michigan Savings Bank, 1903.

George's clairvoyancy got the worst of him when he advised Horace Rackham, the lawyer of Henry Ford, not to invest in the Ford Motor Company, America's biggest car producer.

This 'telephone' has too many shortcomings to be seriously considered as a means of communication.

William Orton, President of Western Union, 1876.

William on Alexander Graham-Bell's latest invention, the telephone, written in an internal memo he sent to colleagues at Western Union.

There's no chance that the iPhone is going to get any significant market share. No chance.

Steve Ballmer, CEO of Microsoft, 2007.

Steve made this comment to *USA Today* and backpedalled out of it two years later admitting he had made a mistake – an understatement if ever there was one.

Rail travel at high speed is not possible, because passengers, unable to breathe, would die of asphyxia.

Dionysius Lardner, Professor of Natural Philosophy & Astronomy, University College London, 1800.

Dionysius' bold claim that high-speed train travel was dangerous was dismissed with the invention of the bullet train in 1964.

66

Everyone acquainted with the subject will recognize it as a conspicuous failure.

99

Henry Morton, president of the Stevens Institute of Technology, 1860.

Thomas Edison's illuminating invention, the light bulb, did not get the approval of Henry Morton. Today, light bulbs are a common household feature.

So many centuries after the Creation, it is unlikely that anyone could find hitherto unknown lands of any value.

A committee advising Spain's King Ferdinand and Queen Isabella of Spain, 1486.

Christopher Columbus asked the Spanish monarchy for funding to travel west to seek new worlds. He went regardless of their committee's findings and, six years later, discovered the Americas.

We have it totally under control. It's one person coming in from China. It's going to be just fine.

Donald Trump, former U.S. President and businessman, January 22, 2020.

Donald's famous last words about coronavirus would come back to haunt him as America would soon be devastated by the virus.

CHAPTER
THREE

ALIVE
AND QUIPPING

History teaches us that funny people are very much alive at the time of their death, metaphorically speaking, of course. Their ability to laugh in the face of their expiration date is worthy of high praise indeed, even if they're evil.

Get your hands ready to applaud these quick-witted comedians not quite ready to leave the stage...

This isn't Hamlet, you know.
It's not meant to go in my
bloody ear.

Laurence Olivier, actor, July 11, 1989.

As the world's once pre-eminent theatre luvvie, Larry
couldn't resist a bit of Shakespearean tragedy in his final
words, spoken to a nurse who supposedly spilled juice
while trying to moisten his lips.

66

The executioner is, I believe, very expert; and my neck is very slender.

99

Queen Anne Boleyn, second wife of Henry VIII, May 19, 1536.

Beheaded on the instructions of her husband, for treason, Anne's sense of gallows humour would be the death of her.

I'd like to be in hell in time for dinner.

Edward H. Rulloff, murderer, May 18, 1871.

Edward was the last person to be hanged in the state of New York. His last words have become a cliché for every movie villain ever since.

Surprise me.

Bob Hope, comedian, July 27, 2003.

When his wife, Dolores, asked him where he wanted to be buried, ever-the-comedian Bob had the perfect parting shot.

Don't worry about it… Look, the clip's not even in it.

Terry Kath, musician, January 23, 1978.

Rock group Chicago's guitarist, Terry died playing a game of Russian Roulette at the actor Don Johnson's house. "What do you think I'm gonna do? Blow my brains out?" Terry said, putting the .38 revolver to his head. The gun was in fact loaded. When he pulled the trigger, Terry died instantly.

"

Doctor, if I put this here guitar down now, I ain't never gonna wake up.

"

Huddie "Leadbelly" Ledbetter, blues musician, December 6, 1949.

Leadbelly left the building for the last time due to Lou Gehrig's disease. He was 61.

66

I would hate to die twice. This dying business is boring.

Richard Feynman, physicist, February 15, 1988.

99

As Richard lay dying from abdominal cancer, the father of quantum mechanics became frustrated, and he said so to his sister, Joan.

It is very beautiful out there.

Thomas Edison, inventor, October 18, 1931.

Moments before his death, light bulb and gramophone inventor Thomas emerged from his coma, opened his eyes and gave his opinion on the view outside his window.

❝

I don't know what I may seem to the world. But as to myself I seem to have been only like a boy playing on the seashore and diverting myself now and then in finding a smoother pebble or a prettier shell than the ordinary, whilst the great ocean of truth lay all undiscovered before me.

❞

Sir Isaac Newton, physicist, March 31, 1727.

On his deathbed, Isaac, discoverer of gravity, among much else, also proved to be a poet.

I am not in the least afraid to die.

Charles Darwin, scientist, April 19, 1882.

The father of the Theory of Evolution, Charles died from heart failure at the age of 73. After studying the origins of life for so long, death seemed only natural.

One never knows the ending.
One has to die to know exactly
what happens after death,
although Catholics have their
hopes.

Alfred Hitchcock, film director, April 29, 1980.

A director with a head for suspense gave his audience one
final twist before he met his maker – he died peacefully in
his sleep.

I want nothing but death.

Jane Austen, author, July 18, 1817.

The *Pride and Prejudice* author had given up on life as she lay on her deathbed, ready for the Hodgkin's lymphoma to take her away. She was 41.

❝

You see, this is how you die.

❞

Coco Chanel, fashion brand icon, January 10, 1971.

At age 87, the famous French fashion designer died as she had lived – in a flourish of fabulousness on her bed in the Ritz, Paris. Her maid Celine recorded her last words.

Goodbye, kid. Hurry back.

Humphrey Bogart, actor, January 14, 1957.

Bogie's last words to his wife, Lauren Bacall, who sat by his deathbed. It's commonly believed his last words were, "I should have never switched from scotch to martinis," but alas, no. He died from oesophageal cancer, aged 57.

I am just going! Have me decently buried; and do not let my body be put into the vault less than three days after I am dead. Do you understand me? … Tis well! I die hard, but I am not afraid to go.

George Washington, first U.S. President, December 14, 1799.

George, who had a fear of being buried alive, died after his doctors drained too much blood from his system (a common practice then) at the age of 67. His last requests were honoured.

What dost thou fear?
Strike man, strike!

Sir Walter Raleigh, English explorer and statesman,
October 29, 1618.

Walter was imprisoned and then beheaded, at the
command of King James I, for treason, upon his return
to England in June 1618.

66

If this is what viral pneumonia does to one, I really don't think I shall bother to have it again.

99

Gladys Cooper, actor, November 17, 1971.

As she looked into a mirror for one last time, Gladys quipped as only Gladys could. She was dead a few hours later.

This is a hell of a way to die.

George S. Patton, U.S. Army general,
December 21, 1945.

After being paralyzed from the neck down due to a car collision, George was told his Army days were over. Sweet relief came when he died peacefully in his sleep that night.

God damn you!

George V, King of the United Kingdom, January 20, 1936.

As revealed by the diary of the king's doctor, Dr Dawson wanted to give the King a more dignified death than dying slowly and painfully from lung disease, so gave him a lethal injection of cocaine and morphine. It's not how George wanted to go.

God bless. Take care of my boy, Roy.

Stan Lee, comic book writer and publisher, November 12, 2018.

The founder of Marvel, Stan died from heart failure. His last words to his son, Roy, were not about another son, rather his most famous creation – Spider-Man.

"

Damn it! Don't you dare ask
God to help me!

"

Joan Crawford, actor, May 10, 1977.

Academy Award-winning star of *Whatever Happened
to Baby Jane?*, Joan's final words were dramatic; she
snapped at her nurse praying loudly at her bedside after
she had a heart attack.

66

Am I dying, or is this my birthday?

99

Lady Nancy Astor, politician, May 2, 1964.

Britain's first female Member of Parliament, whose verbal quarrels with Winston Churchill are legendary, died after suffering a stroke. As she awoke, and saw her family gathered around her bed, she knew her time was up.

❝

And now for a final word from our sponsor.

❞

Charles Gussman, TV and radio writer, October 18, 2000.

Charles always said to his children that he wanted his last words to be memorable. With his health failing on his deathbed, his daughter reminded him of his wish. He slowly removed his oxygen mask and whispered this final, immortal line.

66

I did not know that we had ever quarrelled.

99

Henry David Thoreau, author, May 6, 1862.

Urged to make his peace with God by his physician, Henry's last coherent response was as quick as it was witty. His last actual words were "Moose" and "Indian" and no one knows why.

Here am I, dying of a hundred good symptoms.

Alexander Pope, poet and satirist, May 30, 1744.

Alexander, on the morning of his death, was told by physicians that he was getting better, however the famed poet knew different. He died surrounded by friends.

If all goes well, about a week. If not, about an hour and a half.

Rodney Dangerfield, comedian, October 5, 2004.

Rodney, when asked how long he'll be hospitalised for, following heart surgery, went out with a joke. He never woke up from the operation.

66

Last tag.

99

Richard B. Mellon, industrialist, December 1, 1933.

Richard and his brother Andrew had been playing a game of tag for 70 years. On his deathbed, Richard called his brother over, touched him on the arm and whispered his last words. Andrew remained "it" until his death.

66

What the devil do you mean to sing to me, priest? You are out of tune.

99

Jean-Philippe Rameau, composer,
September 12, 1764.

Suffering from a fever, famed French composer Jean-Philippe's said his final bon mot on his deathbed… and complained to the priest about his terrible singing.

I can't see a damned thing.

Morgan Earp, American lawman, March 18, 1882.

Morgan described what he saw at his time of death, a promise he made to his brother, Wyatt. Wyatt's last words were "Suppose, suppose," when he died in 1929.

That picture is awful dusty.

Jesse James, American outlaw, April 3, 1882.

The last thing on Jesse's mind as he was murdered by Robert Ford paints quite the picture.

I'm ashamed of you, dodging that way. They couldn't hit an elephant at this dist—.

John Sedgwick, general of the Union Army, May 9, 1864.

Shot mid-sentence by a Confederate sharpshooter, the cruel irony behind John Sedgwick's last words will live on. His was one of the Union's highest-ranking deaths during the Civil War.

66

This wallpaper and I are fighting a duel to the death. Either it goes or I do.

99

Oscar Wilde, author and humourist, November 30, 1990.

Lying on his deathbed in a fleapit hotel on the left bank of Paris's River Seine, Oscar, author of *The Picture of Dorian Gray*, quipped this last bit of legendary wit.

Someone else can arrange this.

Constance Spry, pioneering florist and the first domestic goddess, January 3, 1960.

After slipping on stairs while arranging flowers at her home, Constance quipped a phrase for the ages. She died doing what she loved.

Die, my dear? Why, that's the last thing I'll do!

Groucho Marx, comedian, August 19, 1977.

Groucho proved he was alive and quipping right up until the last with this gem. He died of pneumonia in hospital at the age of 86.

CHAPTER
FOUR

FUTURE HISTORY

Predictions of the future are always going to swing in one of two directions – right or wrong. For the poor souls in this chapter, time has not been kind.

However, if you're looking for some awkward examples of self-inflicted word-eating or prophecies that haven't aged well, then turn your attention to these tiny bites of future history…

'Tis but a scratch.

Black Knight, *Monty Python and the Holy Grail* (1975)

Arguably the most famous (if fictional) last words ever to be uttered on the big screen in this comedic masterpiece by the beloved British comedy troupe.

The cinema is little more than a fad. It's canned drama. What audiences really want to see is flesh and blood on the stage.

Charlie Chaplin, actor and director, 1916.

Charlie's own era-defining movies – more than 25 of them – would lead the global expansion of cinema, a fad that may have faltered recently, but has yet to fall.

Who the hell wants to hear actors talk?

Harry Warner, co-founder of Warner Brothers, 1927.

Sound was invented for motion pictures in 1927 and talking has since been universally accepted as the best way to enjoy an actor's performance.

66

There is not the slightest indication that nuclear energy will ever be obtainable. It would mean that the atom would have to be shattered at will.

99

Albert Einstein, physicist, December 29, 1934.

He may have redefined humankind's view of space-time and the universe, but when it came to atoms, Albert didn't see the forest for the trees. Humans went nuclear in 1951.

The subscription model of buying music is bankrupt. I think you could make available the Second Coming in a subscription model, and it might not be successful. 🙰

Steve Jobs, founder of Apple, 2003.

In 2015, Apple Music, the tech giant's subscription model for streaming music, launched and effectively killed the download model, of which Steve was a loyal fan.

No one will pay good money to get from Berlin to Potsdam in one hour when he can ride his horse there in one day for free.

William I, King of Prussia, 1864.

William must have really hated trains for him to get so worked up about them. Alas, their invention spelled the end of long horse rides as a means of transportation.

It will make war impossible.

Hiram Maxim, inventor of the automatic machine gun, 1893.

When asked if his creation will make war more terrible, Hiram's response was so tone-deaf it's ironic because he eventually went deaf after being a little proud of his rather loud invention.

Ours has been the first and, doubtless, will be the last party of whites to visit this profitless locality.

Joseph Ives, Colorado River explorer, April 5, 1858.

While Joe admired the Grand Canyon's breath-taking hugeness, his imagination for its tourism potential was small-scale. Today, it's one of the most visited places on Earth.

How, sir, would you make a ship sail against the wind and currents by lighting a bonfire under her deck? I pray you, excuse me, I have not the time to listen to such nonsense.

Napoleon Bonaparte, French Emperor, 1800.

The great Napoleon, a know-it-all when it came to sea-based naval-gazing, was not a fan of Robert Fulton's latest creation, the steamboat.

The world potential market for copying machines is 5,000 at most.

IBM, inventors of the world's first computer, 1959.

Thankfully, Joseph C. Wilson, one of the founders of Xerox, didn't listen to IBM's ignorance. Photocopiers defined office life for the better part of 50 years, with billions sold.

The Americans have need of the telephone, but the British do not. We have plenty of messenger boys.

Sir William Preece, Chief Engineer at British Post Office, 1878.

When the telephone became a household name by the dawn of the 1900s, and messenger boys grew up into adults, William's was hoisted by his own petard.

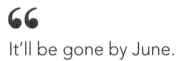

It'll be gone by June.

Variety, music and culture magazine, 1955.

America's original arts magazine made this oft-repeated claim about rock and roll as the genre swept through the nation from sea to shining sea, in the form of Elvis Presley's swingin' hips and blude suede shoes.

It will be years – not in my time – before a woman will become Prime Minister.

Margaret Thatcher, future Prime Minister of Great Britain, October 26, 1969.

It took the Iron Lady 10 years to prove her claim wrong. She became the leader of the nation on May 4, 1979.

You need to get a day job, because you'll never make any money out of children's books.

Barry Cunningham, editor at Bloomsbury Books, 1996.

Barry's advice to JK Rowling is now something she teases him for. Rowling is worth close to £1 billion, with an annual income of £80 million from her wizarding world.

"

Fooling around with alternating current (AC) is just a waste of time. Nobody will use it, ever.

"

Thomas Edison, inventor of the light bulb and Direct Current (DC), 1889.

Thomas and Nikola Tesla's war of the currents became no contest once Tesla's superior AC electricity proved itself with the people. All the people.

There's just not that many videos I want to watch.

Steve Chen, co-founder of YouTube, 2005.

Steve expressed deep concerns about YouTube's long-term viability after it launched, giving rise to the entire video and social streaming industry.

Everyone's always asking me when Apple will come out with a cell phone. My answer is, 'Probably never'.

David Pogue, *The New York Times,* 2006.

David's editorial in his paper remained a (probably) smart remark for about nine months – until Apple launched its first iPhone. The world hasn't been the same since.

If Beethoven's Seventh Symphony is not by some means abridged, it will soon fall into disuse.

Philip Hale, music critic, 1837.

Very few people remember Philip's criticism of Beethoven, but the Seventh Symphony has done a great job of sticking around as, unarguably, the most famous piece of music ever.

66

Far too noisy, my dear Mozart.
Far too many notes.

99

Ferdinand Karl, Emperor of Austria, 1786.

When Emperor Ferdinand attended the first performance of *The Marriage of Figaro*, a world-revered masterpiece by Mozart, the composer was perhaps not expecting such unconstructive criticism.

I'm sorry, Mr Kipling, but you just don't know how to use the English language.

The San Francisco Examiner, 1889.

The Examiner rejected a submission by Rudyard. In 1907, he won the Nobel Prize for Literature. Whoops.

It doesn't matter what he does, he will never amount to anything.

Munich schoolmaster, to Albert Einstein's father, 1885.

When Albert was 10, his teacher described him as "mentally slow, unsociable and adrift forever in his foolish dreams" and was expelled.

Sensible and responsible women do not want to vote.

Grover Cleveland, former U.S. President, 1905.

Today, billions of foolish and irresponsible women get to vote. And the world is a better place for it.

You will be home before the leaves have fallen from the trees.

Kaiser Wilhelm, last German Emperor, August 1914.

After four years of fighting, more than two million German soldiers were killed during WWI – a military and demographic catastrophe, the political, social, economic and cultural consequences of which would precipitate WWII.

"

Taking the best left-handed pitcher in baseball and converting him into a right fielder is one of the dumbest things I ever heard.

"

Tris Speaker, baseball player, 1919.

Tris was talking about Babe Ruth, the greatest American baseball player, who famously began his career as a left-handed pitcher for the Boston Red Sox but became a legend as an outfielder for the New York Yankees.

For the second time in our history, a British Prime Minister has returned from Germany bringing peace with honour. I believe it is peace for our time. We thank you from the bottom of our hearts. Go home and get a nice quiet sleep.

Neville Chamberlain, September 30, 1938.

As Britons slept that night, Adolf Hitler had already reneged on his peace pact with Neville. War with Germany would be declared precisely 11 months later.

That is the biggest fool thing we have ever done. The atomic bomb will never go off, and I speak as an expert in explosives.

William Leahy, admiral, April 13, 1943.

William's appraisal of the Manhattan Project's atomic bomb was short-sighted. When it famously did go off twice, the world was never the same again.

You better get secretarial work
or get married.

Emmeline Snively, director of the Bluebook
Modelling Agency, 1944.

These famous words did not put an end to Norma Jean's
desire to become a model. She changed her name (to
Marilyn Monroe) in 1946 and, well, the rest is herstory.

You ain't goin' nowhere, son.
You ought to go back to drivin'
a truck.

Jimmy Denny, manager of the Grand Ole Opry, 1954.

Jimmy fired Elvis Presley after one performance at
the Grand Ole Opry, offering some wisdom as he did.
Thankfully, Elvis had too much self-belief to listen.

Reagan doesn't have that presidential look.

United Artists executive, 1964.

B-movie actor Ronald Reagan was rejected as the lead star in 1964's *The Best Man* for not having the looks to portray a president convincingly. Ronald, of course, became the actual U.S President in 1981.

People won't want to play these electronic games for more than a week, not once we start selling pinball machines for the home.

Gus Bally, Arcade Inc., 1979.

Pinball machines were a global sensation in the 1970s. But once home computer games came along, they were resigned to history, no matter what Gus thought.

HIV is a pussycat.

Peter Duesberg, Professor of Molecular Biology at
U.C. Berkeley, 1988.

Peter's denial that HIV did not cause AIDS fuelled
misinformation about the virus. Within a decade, more
than 25 million people had died from HIV.

For the most part, the portable computer is a dream machine for the few. On the whole, people don't want to lug a computer with them to the beach or on a train to while away hours they would rather spend reading the sports or business section of the newspaper.

Erik Sandberg-Diment, software columnist for *The New York Times*, 1985.

The perils of predicting the future can be seen in Erik's short-sighted piece about the portable computer. Where to start?

Simply stated, there is no doubt that Saddam Hussein now has weapons of mass destruction.

Dick Cheney, former Vice President of the U.S. August 26, 2002.

Simply stated, there was doubt, Dick. And quite a lot of it. In fact, there were no WMDs.

Next Christmas the iPod will be dead, finished, gone, kaput.

Sir Alan Sugar, businessman, February 2005.

Oh, ye of little faith, Alan. The iPod was launched in 2001 and was only discontinued in 2022, after having sold more than half a billion units.

I see no good reasons why the views given in this volume should shock the religious sensibilities of anyone.

Charles Darwin, author and naturalist, 1869.

Charles's *On the Origin of Species* blew the doors off humanity's history and evolution and effectively pissed off anyone who believed in Intelligent Design, which, at the time, was everyone.

Two years from now, spam will be solved.

Bill Gates, founder of Microsoft, January 26, 2004.

At the World Economic Forum, Bill's bold claim to kill spam has yet to land. Two decades later, it's worse than ever.

To place a man in a multi-stage rocket and project him into the controlling gravitational field of the moon where the passengers can make scientific observations, perhaps land alive, and then return to Earth – all that constitutes a wild dream worthy of Jules Verne... such a man-made voyage will never occur regardless of all future advances.

Lee De Forest, inventor, 1926.

That's precisely what has happened, Lee. Sorry.

66

Based on current trends, probably close to zero new cases in U.S. too by end of April.

99

Elon Musk, Tesla founder, March 6, 2020.

The world's richest man's COVID intelligence is rather poor. To date, there have been 104 million confirmed cases in the U.S. with more than one million deaths. (Worldwide, cases are close to a billion, with more than seven million deaths.)

CHAPTER
FIVE

THE LAST LAUGH

For most of us, our last words will be resigned instantly to the bin of history, mere souvenirs of the mundane, torrid shrieks of pain or asking a family member to "Pass the roast potatoes".

For others, however, the moment of death is merely an opportunity to have the last laugh...

We had a death pact. I have to keep my half of the bargain. Please bury me next to my baby. Bury me in my leather jacket, jeans and motorcycle boots. Goodbye.

Sid Vicious, musician, February 2, 1979.

Sex Pistols' bassist Sid's suicide note was as tragic as his death, and life. His died from a heroin overdose. He was arrested and charged for his girlfriend Nancy's murder, but the case remains unsolved.

66

Thank God, I have done my duty.

99

Horatio Nelson, Royal Navy admiral,
October 21, 1805.

Fatally wounded by gunshot at the Battle of Trafalgar, the
greatest naval battle in history, Horatio died a hero's death
– he won the battle, but the war cost him his life.

Tomorrow at sunrise, I shall no longer be here.

Nostradamus, astrologer and prophet, July 2, 1566.

French predictor of the future, Nostradamus' last insights into his own future turned out to be on the money.
He died as a result of gout. His last words were to his secretary.

She won't think anything
about it.

Abraham Lincoln, former U.S. President,
April 14, 1865.

While enjoying a performance of *Our American Cousin*
at Ford's Theatre, Washington, the president's wife
Mary whispered to him, "What will Miss Harris think of
my hanging on to you so?" (They were holding hands.)
Abe was assassinated seconds later by actor John
Wilkes Booth.

Useless, useless.

John Wilkes Booth, murderer of Abraham Lincoln, April 26. 1885.

Two weeks after he shot President Lincoln in the back, John too was shot by men sent to find him. As he emerged from a flaming barn, gun loaded, bullets pierced his vertebrae. In his dying moment, he asked for his paralyzed arms to be lifted.

No, you certainly can't.

John F. Kennedy, U.S. President, November 22, 1963.

John's wife, Jackie, told the press her husband's last words before Oswald's bullets hit him were to Nellie Connally, the wife of Texas Governor John Connally. She said: "Mr. President, you certainly can't say that Dallas doesn't love you."

Nobody's gonna shoot at me.

Lee Harvey Oswald, assassin, November 24, 1963.

"Famous last words," said James Leavelle, the detective in charge of Lee, moments before JFK's assassin was himself shot by Jack Ruby in a Dallas police station.

I done told you my last request...
a bulletproof vest.

James W. Rodgers, murderer, March 30, 1960.

As he faced a firing squad for the murder of a minor,
James's final wish was denied.

I am sorry to trouble you, chaps.
I don't know how you get along
so fast with the traffic on the road
these days.

Ian Fleming, author, August 12, 1964

Ian, creator of James Bond, quintessentially British to the
end, apologizing to the ambulance paramedics. He died
later at Canterbury Hospital from a heart attack.

Where the hell are the
parachutes?

Glenn Miller, big band leader and US Army Major
during WWII, December 15, 1944.

As he prepared to board a military plane to Paris on a
foggy day, Glenn asked Colonel Norman Baesell a fair
question. Baesell's reply: "What's the matter, Miller, don't
you want to live forever?" Miller, and the plane, vanished
into thin air.

I've said all I've had to say.

Bill Hicks, comedian, February 14, 1994.

One of America's biggest and best-loved alternative comics, Bill died from pancreatic cancer 11 days after his last words. However, he voluntarily stopped speaking after saying these final last words. He was just 32.

Jesus, Jesus, Jesus!

Joan of Arc, patron saint of France, May 30, 1341.

Nineteen-year-old Joan's divine inspiration ended when she was burned at the stake for heresy, despite leading the French army to victory at Orléans and stopping England's conquering of France.

This is important.

Albert Einstein, physicist, April 18, 1955.

The world's biggest brain spoke his (disputed) last words when he awoke from surgery, in German, to his secretary, who didn't understand German too well. To this day, scientists joke about whether what he said was crucial to the meaning of the universe – now lost forever.

"

I'm not, but I'd rather be skiing.

"

Stan Laurel, comedian, February 23, 1965.

Just before he died, Stan told his hospital nurse he would like to go skiing. The nurse was surprised. "Are you a skier, Mr Laurel?" she said, prompting his reply.

Say goodbye to Pat. Say goodbye to Jack. And say goodbye to yourself, because you're a nice guy.

Marilyn Monroe, actress, August 4, 1962.

Marilyn's last words were while on the phone to actor Peter Lawson. Jack is JFK. She was slurring her words, after an apparent overdose of barbiturates. She was just 36.

66

I am just going outside and may be some time.

99

Lawrence Oates, Antarctica explorer, March 17, 1912.

Trapped in a tent and too weak and cold to continue their Terra Nova Expedition, Oates left his team and walked out into a blizzard. His body was never found.

66

The ladies have to go first.
Get into the lifeboat, to please
me. Good bye, dearie. I'll see
you later.

99

John Jacob Astor IV, businessman, April 15, 1912.

John, the wealthiest passenger aboard the *Titanic*,
ensured his pregnant wife made it aboard one of the
sinking ship's lifeboats. He remained aboard the
Titanic. Both sunk to their watery grave.

Don't turn on the light.

Osama bin Laden, Al-Qaeda leader, May 1, 2011.

Ten years after the events of 9/11, a U.S. Navy Seal team shot dead the man responsible in his bed in his Pakistan compound. Bin Laden's last words were to his one of his wives.

66

I need help bad, man.

99

Jimi Hendrix, musician, September 18, 1970.

Jimi called his manager, Chas Chandler, and left these chilling words on his answering machine. He died soon after he aspirated his own vomit and died of asphyxia, while intoxicated with barbiturates.

Don't worry, they usually don't swim backwards… I'm dying.

Steve Irwin, conservationist, September 4, 2006.

Australian wildlife hero and TV star died after a stingray barb pierced his chest. Steve said these words to his cameraman, whose camera captured the moment, when he knew the creature had killed him.

Good night, Malaysian three-seven-zero.

Zaharie Ahmad Shah, airline pilot, March 8, 2014.

As captain of Malaysia Airlines Flight 370, Ahmad's final transmission is one of the most mysterious sign-offs in human history. The plane was never heard from again.

❝
Well, boys, do your best for the women and children, and look out for yourselves.
❞

Edward Smith, captain of the RMS *Titanic*, April 15, 1912.

Edward's last orders to the *Titanic's* crew members after it struck the iceberg. He went down with the ship.

66

It is nothing... it is nothing...

99

Franz Ferdinand, archduke of Austria, June 28, 1914.

On his way to hospital after being fatally shot by a Serbian nationalist, Franz was confident his wound was but a scratch. His death was more than nothing – it was the first domino that started World War I.

66

France, the army, head of the army, Joséphine.

99

Napoleon Bonaparte, first emperor of France,
May 5, 1821.

France's greatest military leader died from stomach cancer
(or possible poisoning) while in exile due to his failed
invasion of Russia. His last words were a list of the things
he loved most.

When I put out my hands this way, then. Stay for the sign.

King Charles I, King of England, February 2, 1626.

At the end of a lengthy speech on the chopping block, King Charles I was executed for high treason. His last words were to his executioner and told him when to drop the axe. "Yes, I will, and it please Your Majesty," the axeman said before cutting off his head.

Pardon me, sir. I did not do it on purpose.*

Marie Antoinette, last Queen of France, October 16, 1973.

While France starved, treasonous Marie, and husband King Louis XVI of France, were sentenced to die by guillotine. Before the blade fell, she accidentally stepped on the executioner's foot. Her apology (in French) was said just before she lost her head.

*"Pardonnez-moi, monsieur. Je ne l'ai pas fait exprès."

How's this for your headline?
'French Fries!'

James Donald French, American criminal,
August 10, 1966.

Convicted murderer, and the last criminal ever to be
executed in Oklahoma, French's last words were as
funny as they were unremorseful. He was electrocuted
seconds later.

Sorry for saying fuck.

Graham Chapman, comedian, October 4, 1989.

Chapman was apologizing to his nurse, who had earlier injected him, as he passed. At Graham's funeral, John Cleese delivered a eulogy and became the first person to say "fuck" during a televized memorial service. Chapman would have approved.

66

You too, child?

99

Julius Caesar, Roman dictator, March 15, 44 BCE.

Julius was stabbed 23 times on the day he was assassinated by a group of men. His stepson Brutus's cut probably felt the deepest, as these (often disputed) last words were uttered at him.

Are you guys ready? Let's roll.

99

Todd Beamer, passenger on United Airlines Flight 93,
September 11, 2001.

All 44 passengers died onboard Flight 93, en route to
Washington D.C, but not before a revolt against the
flight's Al-Qaeda hijackers – led by Todd – forced them to
crash-land in Pennsylvania.

"

Olivia, you'll be fine, you'll be fine…

"

George Harrison, musician, November 29, 2001.

With his wife Olivia and son, Dhani, by his deathbed, George's being slipped into the greater conscious of the universe. Olivia would later tell the press that George's favourite phrase was, "Everything else can wait, but the search for God cannot wait, and love one another," and he said this shortly before he died.

66

That was a great game of golf,
fellas. Let's get a Coke.

99

Bing Crosby, actor and entertainer, October 14, 1977.

Against doctors' orders, Bing continued to play golf. After
18 holes at the La Moraleja Golf Course, Madrid, which
Bing won (with a card of 85), he lost the rhythm of his
heart on his return to the clubhouse. He was 74.

Pity, pity, too late!*

Ludwig van Beethoven, composer,
March 26, 1827.

Ludwig's last recorded words suggest the diagnosis of
his death – liver failure. Ludwig loved to drink and when
a publisher sent him 12 bottles of wine as a gift, the
composer knew he would be dead before they arrived.
He fell into a coma and died two days later.

*"Schade, schade, zu spät!"

The earth is suffocating... Swear to make them cut me open, so that I won't be buried alive.

Frédéric Chopin, composer, October 17, 1849.

Fred's fear of being buried alive was a fear held by many in his time. Instead, Chopin died of tuberculosis at the age of 39. His last words were an instruction to his sister to remove his heart and bury it and not, "Now is my final agony. No more," while listening to Mozart's Requiem.

Better, my friend, I can feel the daisies growing over me.

John Keats, poet, February 23, 1821.

On his deathbed, in Rome, riddled with tuberculosis, John was asked by his friend Joseph Severn how he was doing. His reply was his last.

God bless you! Is that you, Dora?

William Wordsworth, poet, April 23, 1850.

William uttered this immortal line on his deathbed, dying from pleurisy, a vision of his daughter, Dora, who had died three years earlier. His days wandering lonely as a cloud were over.

Take away these pillows, I won't need them any longer.

Lewis Carroll, author, January 14, 1898.

Charles Lutwidge Dodgson, or Lewis Carroll as he was known following *Alice's Adventures in Wonderland*, died of pneumonia.

"

And if you don't like it, you can fuck off.

"

Keith Moon, drummer for The Who,
7 September 1978.

After dining with Paul McCartney in London, Keith went back to his flat with girlfriend Annette Walter-Lax. He demanded she make him steak and eggs, but she refused. When she returned, Keith was dead.

No. (In sign language)

Alexander Graham Bell, inventor, August 2, 1922.

Lying on his deathbed, Alexander's beloved wife Mabel – whose deafness inspired him to experiment with soundwaves and invent the telephone – pleaded with her husband, "Don't leave me."

Who is it? Who is it?

William H. Bonney, a.k.a. Billy the Kid, July 14, 1881.

Outlaw Billy the Kid boasted of shooting dead 21 men before he was 21. Before he died, Billy wanted to know who (out of his many enemies) took him down. It was Sheriff Pat Garrett.

66

I'm in the fourth quarter, and
I need you to get me out of
the game.

99

Chadwick Boseman, actor, August 28, 2020.

Chad's last words, to his pastor-brother Derrick, alerted
his family to the fact the *Black Panther* actor was ready
to succumb to the colon cancer the world knew nothing
about.

"

Well, I've got to be alive for it, haven't I?

"

Prince Philip, Prince Consort to Elizabeth II, April 9, 2021.

Philip's last words to his son, the future King of England, Charles, were about Philip's 100th birthday. He died an hour or so later, two months and one day shy of his century.

66

Have I played the part well?
Then applaud as I exit.

99

Augustus, First Emperor of Rome, August 19, 14 AD.

Augustus was the founder of the Roman Empire, and
nephew of Julius Caesar. He died from an unknown illness.

Drink to me, drink to my health,
you know I can't drink anymore.

Pablo Picasso, artist, April 8, 1973.

The night before he died in his sleep, after suffering a
pulmonary edema, Pablo entertained friends at his French
chateau. Before he went to bed, he said his piece.

Remember, Honey, don't forget what I told you. Put in my coffin a deck of cards, a mashie niblick, and a pretty blonde.

Chico Marx, comedian, October 11, 1961.

Chico's last words were instructions to his wife, Mary. His body lies now in a crypt in California. Contents unknown.

Your Queen is sending you to the Tower!

Elizabeth II, Queen of Great Britain,
September 8, 2022.

Elizabeth's light-hearted quip to Dr Iain Greenshields, who was staying at the Tower of London, was uttered during one of her last conversations before she died of old age. She was 96.

66

Hasta la vista, baby.

99

Boris Johnson, UK Prime Minister, July 20, 2022.

Boris's final words in the House of Commons as PM hinted a return. Since his departure, the Partygate scandal, among many other controversies, has continued to engulf his plans in flames.